The SEQUENCE to ALIGNED WEALTH

WORKBOOK

THIS WORKBOOK BELONGS TO

_____

The SEQUENCE to ALIGNED WEALTH

WORKBOOK

Companion to the book *The Sequence to Aligned Wealth* by Christina Ostroski

THE SEQUENCE TO ALIGNED WEALTH WORKBOOK

2025 ChristinaOstroski

Copyright © 2025 Christina Ostroski

All rights reserved. No part of this book may be reproduced, scanned, or distributed in any printed or electronic form without permission. No portion of this book may be used in any alternative manner whatsoever without express written consent from the publisher/author.

The author in this book has made every effort to ensure the accuracy of the information they have provided at the time of publication. The author does not assume and hereby disclaims any liability to any party for loss, damage, or disruption caused by errors or omissions, whether such errors or omissions were from accident, negligence, or any other cause. This book is not intended as legal, financial, or therapeutic advice. Always consult a qualified professional. This book is not a replacement for medical advice from a registered physician.

The publisher is not responsible for websites, social media, or other content that is not owned by the publisher.

ISBN Paperback: 978-1-7774334-5-1

www.christinaostroski.com

Christina OSTROSKI

HOW TO USE THIS WORK BOOK

This workbook is the hands-on companion to *The Sequence to Aligned Wealth*. It is designed to help you move from reading to doing — page by page, step by step. It's built for action, reflection, and results.

Each section of this workbook follows the **W.E.A.L.T.H. framework.** You'll see the same structure, exercises, and prompts as the book, but here you'll have the space to apply it directly to your own life and add reminders, notes or any aha moments you want to come back to in the future.

- On the left-hand page, you'll find the prompts, exercises, and tools taken from the book.

- On the right-hand page, you'll find lined space for your reflections, notes, breakthroughs, and anything you want to capture. Use it freely — write, brainstorm, and repeat the exercises as often as needed.

- Move section by section (W, E, A, L, T, H) to stay aligned and focused while reading the book.

- This workbook is the perfect side-by-side if you want to keep your main book clean to gift, revisit, or preserve for the future.

This is your space to experiment, think differently, and commit your wealth journey to paper. The more you write and reflect, the more powerful these exercises become.

Don't just read wealth — live it, write it, own it.

SEQUENCE TO ALIGNED WEALTH ROADMAP

WITHIN   ELICIT   ATTRACT   LANGUAGE   THOUGHT-CATHCING   HEAL

W — Within
Step into your wealthiest self. This is about your self-concept, inner abundance, and the identity of the version of you who already has it all. Here we focus on self-discovery, power, and building a rich mindset from the inside out.

E — Elicit
Feel it first. Learn to bring up the emotions and energy that match your goals. Identify the beliefs and behaviors blocking your money flow and shift into a higher wealth frequency.

A — Attract
When your energy, thoughts, and actions align, wealth is drawn to you. This is where you lock in your desires and stay in the flow that pulls prosperity your way.

L — Language
Words shape your world. Shift your "I am" statements and internal language to support confidence, money, and success. Create a new story that builds your wealthy identity.

T — Thought Catching
Catch the thoughts running on autopilot. Notice what limits you, interrupt it, and rewire your mind to support clarity, confidence, and financial growth.

H — Heal
Release what weighs you down—shame, guilt, past money wounds. Reframe emotional debts and let go of what keeps you stuck so you can move forward free and powerful.

W

Within

The version of you who has stepped into your wealthiest self — the fullest expression of who you are as a limitless, magical being.

MAKE IT REAL

Write your answers to make this exercise more impactful.

Ask Yourself:

Who in your life would be **directly impacted** if you became wealthy beyond your wildest imagination?

List the ways your financial success could change their lives:

- **Your partner:** How?
- **Your parents:** How?
- **Your siblings:** How?
- **Your extended family:** How?
- **Your friends:** How?
- **Your employees:** How?
- **Anyone else?** Who and how?

Now close your eyes and **imagine** it —
Scenarios where your wealth positively impacts the people around you.

What if...?

If you had the wealth that you desire, you could do whatever you want with it. What would happen, what would you do, and who would it impact?

This is your permission slip to go all in!

WEALTH NOTES

THE FIVE TYPES OF WEALTH

There are five key areas that shape a wealthy life:

1. Financial Wealth
2. Time Wealth
3. Physical Wealth
4. Social Wealth
5. Spiritual Wealth

Ask yourself:
- Where am I wealthy right now?
- Where am I barely scraping by?
- What's costing me more than it's giving?

That's the level of honesty that changes everything.

When all five align, wealth stops being something you chase.

It becomes the way you live.

Wealth Notes

STOP CHEATING ON YOUR MONEY

Let's think about where this idea of hard work equals money really came from.

I want you to think about who taught you Your Money Story?

1. Where did it come from?

2. How were you raised?

3. Who taught you those beliefs?

Your money mindset often stems from lessons learned from trusted figures or past experiences that slipped out of your control.

These beliefs, however well-intentioned, might be holding you back. It's time to align energetically with the wealth you seek, embodying the confidence of someone who knows they can have it all.

Wealth Notes

UNCOVER & SHIFT

Here's a powerful exercise to uncover and shift your deep-seated beliefs, not just about money, but all areas of your life.

1. Grab a journal or open a voice memo app.

2. I'll prompt you with a statement and you'll immediately jot down or verbalize your gut reaction. Write or speak your thoughts as they come.

3. Once you've recorded your response, take a moment to reflect. Seeing or hearing your unfiltered thoughts can be eye-opening.

4. Don't rush to fix everything at once. Aim to address one belief or thought pattern at a time.

5. While we're talking about money here, this method works across the board—your relationships, self-image, finances, all of it. It's a go-to tool for growth, no matter where you use it.

I want you to think of what your first memories of money were?

-Is it asking your parents for pizza money for school, getting a birthday card in the mail from a relative, asking for change for the candy store, bus fare, raising money for school fundraisers, parents figuring out bills at the table, friends asking to borrow money for cafeteria food.

Don't edit or judge your response; just let it flow naturally, capturing it precisely as it emerges, free from any notions of right or wrong.

Got it? Great. Proceed on the next page

Wealth Notes

Money is _____.

Money really is _____.

People who have a lot of money are _____.

People who don't have a lot of money are _____.

Money creates _____.

I would make more money if _____.

Rich people are rich because _____.

Poor people are poor because _____.

My mom thought money was _____.

My dad thought money was _____.

My high school friends viewed people with money as _____.

My college friends viewed people with money as _____.

My current friends view people with money as _____.

Money makes people _____.

I think money can _____.

I'm afraid money will make me _____.

If I had more money, I would _____.

If I did better than my partner financially then _____.

If I did better than my colleagues financially then _____.

Wealth Notes

If I did better than my father financially then _____.

If I did better than my mother financially then _____.

The best way you can spend money is _____.

The worst way you can spend money is _____.

I would never spend money on _____.

I could never afford to _____.

I would judge people if they used their money for _____.

I should spend my money on _____.

When people who are wealthier than me talk about money, I feel _____.

When people who are less wealthy than me talk about money, I feel _____.

If I could teach people one thing about money, it would be that _____.

I would feel comfortable with $_____ in my bank account.

I would feel uncomfortable with $_____ in my bank account.

I currently have $_____ in my bank account.

Use the Wealth Notes section to expand on your answers.

WEALTH NOTES

RECOGNIZE & ACKNOWLEDGE

To change money scripts, start by recognizing and acknowledging them.

Here's a step-by-step guide:

1. Awareness: The first step is recognizing the existing money scripts. You've already begun this by identifying what thoughts and beliefs you have around money.

2. Reflection: Reflect on where these beliefs come from. Consider your upbringing, influential people in your life, experiences, and societal messages about money.

3. Challenge and Question: For each belief, ask yourself, "Is this really true? Does this belief serve my current goals and lifestyle? Where did it come from, and is it based on my reality or someone else's fears or experiences?"

4. Rewrite Your Narrative: Create new, empowering beliefs. For example, if your old script is, "Money is the root of all evil," you might reframe it as, "Money is a tool for doing great things in the world."

5. Action: Align your actions with your new beliefs. This could mean making financial decisions that reflect your new mindset, like spending in a way that brings you joy and aligns with your values.

6. Consistency and Patience: Changing deeply ingrained beliefs takes time and consistent effort. Regularly remind yourself of your new beliefs and why they are important to you.

7. Celebrate Progress: Recognize and celebrate changes in your financial behavior and mindset, no matter how small. This reinforces positive change and motivates you to continue.

WEALTH NOTES

MYTHS ABOUT MONEY

Myth 1: Money is the Root of All Evil
Let's kick things off with a classic: 'Money is the root of all evil.' Now, I'm not sure who came up with this gem, but let's set the record straight. Money itself isn't evil. Nope, not one bit. It's just a tool, like a hammer or a knife. It's all about how you use it that counts.

Myth 2: You Need Money to Make Money
Ah, the age-old saying, "You need money to make money." Sure, having some cash to invest can give you a leg up, but let me tell you a little secret: it's not the only way to get ahead. In fact, some of the most successful people out there started with nothing but a dream and some hustle.

Myth 3: The Rich Get Richer, and the Poor Get Poorer
Now, this one's a real doozy. "The rich get richer, and the poor get poorer." Sounds pretty bleak, right? Well, I'm here to tell you it's not set in stone. Certainly, there are challenges that can make it more difficult for some individuals to succeed, but that doesn't mean it's game over.

Myth 4: Money Can't Buy Happiness
Last but not least, we've got the age-old saying, "Money can't buy happiness." Now, I'll admit, there's some truth to this one. Money alone won't magically make all your problems disappear. It sure can make life a lot easier, though. The truth is that money can't buy the emotion of happiness itself, but it can buy the things, experiences, comfort, and security that contribute to happiness.

What money myths have you heard? And now that you know the truth, how will you shut them down for good?

Wealth Notes

SWIPE RIGHT FOR WEALTH

Let's break down what makes your money relationship either powerful or exhausting.

- Think about all the different relationships in your life, like with your friends, family, co-workers, or partner. What's your idea of a fantastic, empowering relationship? What are the must-haves for you to feel supported and positive in these relationships? Now, think about what definitely shouldn't be there. What are the big no-nos or things that just ruin a relationship for you, whether it's with a buddy or your significant other?

- When you think about the relationships in your life that just suck the energy out of you, what comes to mind? Describe what a negative or disempowering relationship looks like for you. What elements make it feel toxic or just plain bad? And on the flip side, what's usually missing in these relationships that leaves you feeling down?

- Our relationship with money often mirrors our interactions with people in our lives. It's like holding up a mirror to how we connect with others and how we handle our finances. Do you notice a connection between how you treat your relationships and how you manage money? For example, if you neglect spending quality time with your personal connections, could you also be neglecting your financial planning? Or if you shy away from difficult discussions with friends or family, do you also avoid facing financial issues head-on? What patterns do you see between your social and financial behaviors?

Wealth Notes

SWIPE RIGHT FOR WEALTH...CONT.

- When conversations around money come up, do you shrink or expand? Is it constant with anyone you're talking to, or does it change based on the other person's financial "status"?

- How much time do you spend thinking about money? What are your thoughts about it? Are they loving and grateful? Or stressed and frantic?

- Does money keep you up at night? Does it make you unable to sleep or eat?

- If I were to ask you to go into your bank account and look at your money, what comes up? How do you feel?

- Beyond your survival and basic needs, what do you desire money for? What will you do with it? In the present moment? In the future? (family stuff, home, luxury, experiences, travel, hobbies, self-care, health, charity, etc.)

- As you write those desires out, what thoughts, beliefs, reactions, judgments, or feelings are coming up for you?

- How can having more money allow you to contribute even more to the world and be more generous? What will you do as you make more and more money? Where do you want to give back?

Wealth Notes

SWIPE RIGHT FOR WEALTH...CONT.

- Imagine if you could dive into the most captivating relationship with money ever. I'm not just talking about some fleeting infatuation; I'm talking about a soul-deep connection that's rich, expansive, and fulfilling AF. How would that look and feel like for you? Picture the long-lasting and nourishing bond you crave with money. When you're dealing with it day in and day out, how do you want to feel? What expectations do you hold for this money romance, and how do you plan to have each other's backs? Let's dish—what's your dream money relationship all about?

- What's missing in your current relationship with money that shows up in your ideal money relationship?
-
- What's present in your current money relationship that you don't want in your ideal one?
-
- What needs to change to bring you closer to your ideal money relationship? What's your first move?

- What are your tendencies and habits with money? Do you spend it all—on yourself, on others, both? Do you "hoard" it?

Wealth Notes

If you save money for a "rainy day..."

- What does that mean to you? Describe what you envision a "rainy day" to be in terms of your finances.

- Think about the reasons someone might save money for a "rainy day." What do you believe are the benefits of having a financial safety net?

- Reflect on your own habits and attitudes toward saving money for unexpected expenses. Do you currently set aside funds for emergencies or unforeseen circumstances? Why or why not?

- Consider the emotions associated with saving money for a "rainy day." How does the idea of having a financial cushion make you feel? Are there any anxieties or uncertainties that come up?

- Imagine a scenario where you need to dip into your savings for a "rainy day." How would you feel about using that money? What criteria would you use to determine when it's appropriate to access those funds?

Wealth Notes

If you save money for a "rainy day..."cont...

- Explore the concept of preparedness versus over-caution for saving for a "rainy day." How do you balance being smart with your money and still living your life right now?

- Think about the impact of saving for a "rainy day" on your overall financial well-being. How does having a financial safety net affect your sense of security and peace of mind?

- Consider how your upbringing or experiences may have influenced your approach to saving money for unexpected expenses. Are there any beliefs or attitudes inherited from family or learned through personal experience?

Saving for a rainy day is a common piece of advice, but it can hold you back if it turns into fear-driven hoarding or keeps you from investing and growing your wealth.

Finding your own balance between safety and growth is where the real power lies.

These prompts should help stimulate deeper reflection on the concept of saving for a "rainy day" and its significance in

WEALTH NOTES

But, if you spend your money right away...

- Reflect on your spending habits. Do you spend money as soon as you receive it? What motivates this behaviour?

- Consider the immediate gratification of spending money versus the long-term benefits of saving or investing it. How do you weigh these two options when making financial decisions?

- Explore any emotions or impulses that arise when you have money available to spend. Do you feel a sense of urgency or excitement about making purchases? How do these feelings impact your spending patterns?

- Think about the consequences of spending money impulsively. Have you ever regretted a purchase made on a whim? What lessons have you learned from these experiences?

- Consider the role of budgeting and financial planning in managing your spending habits. Do you have a budget in place to help prioritize your expenses and allocate funds wisely?

As you review your answers, some surprising insights might emerge. What's coming up as you dive deeper into your thoughts and feelings about money? Jot down any revelations or shifts in perspective; this is all part of your journey to a stronger, more empowered money relationship.

Wealth Notes

HOW MONEY SHOWS UP IN RELATIONSHIPS

- When money comes up, do you puff up like a peacock or shrink like a raisin in the sun?

- Does the way you talk about money shift depending on who's flashing the cash?

- How much headspace does money rent in your brain?

- Are your thoughts about it all lovey-dovey or more like a stressed-out parent at a kid's birthday party?

- Does money keep you up at night, tossing and turning, or worse, snacking?

- When you jump on Google looking for quick fixes or how-tos about money, what are you googling?

- If I dared you to peek into your bank account right now, what would you see? Go on, feel those heart palpitations.

- Beyond the essentials, what's your money mojo for? Dreaming of luxury yachts or just paying off student loans?

- As you pen down those desires, what's popping up in your head? Guilt? Excitement? A sudden craving for chocolate?

- How can stacking more dough make you the superhero of philanthropy?

- Where do you want to make it rain when the cash flow increases?

Investing in a better relationship is a necessity for kicking your Wealthy Life into high gear!

WEALTH NOTES

Have a Heart-to-Heart with Money

Here's an example letter:

Dear Money, Okay, real talk. We've had a complicated relationship. I've blamed you, chased you, ignored you, obsessed over you, and honestly, treated you like crap. One minute I'm desperate for you, the next I'm pushing you away like you're the villain in some twisted drama I wrote in my head.

My stress, shame, guilt, and worth, I've made you responsible. I expected you to fix everything, then got mad when you didn't show up. I've judged people who had a lot of you, and I've
judged myself for not having enough. That ends now. I am so sorry.

I'm not here to beg or play victim. I'm owning my part. I've made you the enemy when really, you've just been waiting for me to get my shit together and treat you right.

So here it is, I'm sorry.

I'm sorry for talking shit about you. I'm sorry for acting like you're never enough. I'm sorry for not trusting you to stick around. I'm sorry for using you as a measuring stick for my value. I'm sorry for thinking you only show up when I hustle myself into the ground. I'm sorry for not seeing you as the generous, powerful, neutral force you are.

From now on, I'm choosing something different. I'm choosing respect. Partnership. Appreciation. I'll pay attention. I'll make room for you. I'll let you flow without gripping so tight. No more toxic patterns. No more hot-and-cold energy. Just truth, clarity, and trust. You're not the problem. You never were. I was just scared to receive you without conditions. But I'm done playing small.

Let's rewrite this story together.
Love,
Me

Express yourself however feels right, whether it's a formal letter or just a casual talk. The point is to lean into this exercise fully and see what truths come up about your money relationship.

Happy writing!

WEALTH NOTES

Write a letter to money

Imagine money is sitting right across from you, like a trusted friend, ready for a heart-to-heart chat. I want you to write a letter to money, pouring out your thoughts, feelings, and intentions about your relationship with it. Be honest, be vulnerable, and let it all out.

WEALTH NOTES

Write a letter from money

Once you've written your letter to money, I want you to flip the script. Now, imagine money is responding to you. What would it say? Write a letter from your perspective, addressing your concerns, acknowledging your efforts, and offering your perspective on your relationship.

Wealth Notes

WEALTH FROM WITH

Ask yourself, "Who is the person who gets the result?" What do they think? What are their beliefs? Their most common feelings are what? Who do they BE? If you already had $10K sitting in your account, what would you be doing right now? Would you move differently? Make bolder choices? Stop stressing over little things?

Who are you as the version of you who knows you're infinitely rich in every area of life and has the power to create what you truly want?

Before moving forward, tap into your wealthy self. This is the version of you who knows they're rich in every part of life. The big-picture, whole-person you who fully owns wealth from within.

Ask yourself:

- What does your wealthy life look like?
- What is the energy of your wealthy self?
- What are your wealthy traits and qualities?
- What are you available for and ready to open yourself up to?
- What are you no longer available for and releasing?
- What are your values?
- How do you dress?
- What is your day like?
- How do you interact with people?
- What do you invest your time, money, and energy in?

Wealth Notes

Now let's go deeper with embodiment.

This is about stepping into the version of you who already has what you want. It's reverse-engineering from that outcome. This part is more targeted and practical.

Try this on for size:

- What is the thing you desire to have?
- Who is the person who already has what it is you desire?
- What are their thoughts and beliefs?
- What are their predominant feelings?
- What are the actions they take?
- What do they do regularly?

Do you see how this differs from how you are currently being and doing?

What is the biggest thing that needs to shift?

Take a minute to journal on who your wealthy self is and how you can tap into that power starting now.

WEALTH NOTES

Let's go a little deeper into meeting the wealth from within.

Describe your wealthy self from when they wake up to when they go to bed, answering the following questions on a subconscious level -the first thing that comes to mind.

Who is your wealthy self?

The version of you who knows they're infinite and can create whatever they desire.

What is the energy of your wealthy self?

What vibe do they carry? Calm? Powerful? Magnetic?

What time do you wake up?

Is it early and intentional or slow and luxurious?

Describe your bed.

Is it big, soft, and full of pillows? Does it face a window? What color is the bedding? What do you see, hear, and feel when you wake up?

Where are you?

Are you in a city condo, a beach house, on a lake, an island, in the mountains, on a yacht, or in your dream home?

Wealth Notes

Let's go a little deeper into meeting the wealth from within...cont.

Who's with you?
Are you alone, with a partner, family, friends, or pets?

How do you feel when you wake up?
Energized? Grateful? Excited? At peace?

How do you dress?
What's your style? What fabrics, colors, or pieces make you feel wealthy?

What are you having for breakfast?
Where and what are you eating? What does the setting feel like?

What does your morning look like?
Are you doing yoga, meditating, journaling, walking, or reading?

What do your meals look, taste, and feel like?
Are they fresh, fancy, slow, indulgent? Where are you eating—out, home, patio?

Wealth Notes

Let's go a little deeper into meeting the wealth from within...cont.

What does your afternoon look like?

Are you meeting friends for coffee, going to the spa, shopping, reading, or relaxing?

Who do you surround yourself with?

What people are in your circle? Uplifting? Ambitious? Fun?

What is your day like?

What's your flow from start to finish? Are you working, creating, playing, or leading?

How do you interact with people?

Are you confident, kind, magnetic, calm, or direct?

How do you move through the day?

Do you walk with purpose, ease, or energy?

How do you celebrate?

Small wins? Big ones? Do you treat yourself? Share joy with others?

Wealth Notes

Let's go a little deeper into meeting the wealth from within...cont.

What does your evening look like?
Is it movie night, making a beautiful dinner, stargazing, time with loved ones?

What are you doing right before bed?
Are you meditating, journaling, stretching, winding down with tea? What time is it?

What were you grateful for when you went to bed the night before?
What moments stood out?

Can you visualize and feel yourself living this?

Is it vivid and clear? (if not, tweak the image in your mind until it actually hits.)

See what you would see, hear what you would hear, and feel all the feelings!

Take some time to journal about who your wealthy self is and how you can tap into that power now.

Wealth Notes

THE BE, DO, HAVE MODEL

BE	DO	HAVE
Create a way of BEing in alignment with your goal	Your way of BEing will propel you into action	The results of your actions will bring YOU to your goal

The Be-Do-Have model is a simple yet powerful framework for achieving your goals and manifesting your desires.

Ask yourself, "Who's the person who gets the result?" What do they think? What do they believe? What are their strongest feelings? Who are they BE-ing? As the person who already has $20k in their bank account, what would they be doing? When you BE and then DO while fully embodying that BE-ing, you end up HAVING what YOU desire.

Give this a try:)

- What is the thing you desire to have or the result you want to create?

- Who is the person who already has what you desire?

- What are their thoughts and beliefs?

- What are their strongest or most important feelings?

- What actions do they take? What do they do regularly?

Do you see how this differs from the way you are currently being and doing?

What is the biggest thing that needs to shift for you to uplevel—your money mindset, your beliefs, your story, your identity, how you relate to money, your relationship with it?

Wealth Notes

Wealth Notes

WEALTH NOTES

WEALTH NOTES

E

Elicit

Bring out the emotions and energy of your goals, one step at a time, and embody the feeling of already having them.

DIVINE DESIRE

Divine Desire sets the vision, Top Outcome Goals mark the milestones, and Process Goals are the consistent actions that get you there.

Start by locking in your **Divine Desire,** then break it into clear **outcome goals** that move you forward step by step.

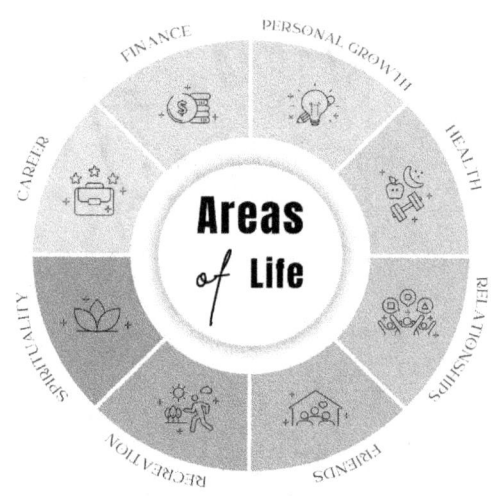

What Each Area really Means

HEALTH
Fitness
Sleep
Nutrition
Self-Care
Wellness

RELATIONSHIPS
Connection
Love
Support
Communication
Intimacy

FRIENDS
Quality Time
Bonding
Laughter
Support
Community

PERSONAL GROWTH
Mindset Work
Education
Learning
Reading
Reflection

CAREER
Purpose
Clients
Workload
Fulliment
Leadership

RECREATION
Play
Hobbies
Adventures
Leisure
Joy

FINANCE
Income
Budgeting
Spending
Savings
Investments

SPIRITUALITY
Nature
Source
Faith
Giving Back
Gratitude

WEALTH NOTES

IDENTIFY THE BIG VISION FOR YOUR LIFE

Think big and limitless as you consider these questions. Imagine all the endless possibilities waiting for you.

- If no one's judgment or side-eyes could touch you, what bold thing would you bring into the world that's guaranteed to rock?

- What wild dreams are you hiding deep inside — the ones you haven't even dared to whisper to yourself?

- If you could guarantee your own success and build your perfect world, what would it look like? What would make you feel truly amazing?

_____

_____

_____

_____

_____

_____

_____

_____

WEALTH NOTES

Now, ground those big visions into specifics.

Ask yourself:

- When you think about the bigger vision for your life, what is it you desire?

- What's the legacy you want to leave?

- What's your 5-year goal?

- Your 1-year goal?

- What are your 3–6 month goals?

- What are your top goals and desires for this book's experience?

Wealth Notes

UNCOVER YOUR DIVINE DESIRE

Step 1: Lock In Your Outcome Goals

For each area of life, write 1–3 outcome goals—the big results you want to create in the next 3–6 months. Think of outcome goals as the end game or what success looks like. If anything was possible (spoiler: it is), what would you make happen?

Heads up: I'll explain the "Rate Yourself" column in Step 2. Leave it blank for now!

You don't need to fill in every category right away. Start with the areas that feel most important to you now, then expand over time.

Finances

Rate Yourself	Outcome Goals
	1. 2. 3.

Health + Wellness

Rate Yourself	Outcome Goals
	1. 2. 3.

WEALTH NOTES

Personal Growth & Spirituality

Rate Yourself	Outcome Goals
	1. 2. 3.

Relationships (Partnership, Family, Friends)

Rate Yourself	Outcome Goals
	1. 2. 3.

Career / Business

Rate Yourself	Outcome Goals
	1. 2. 3.

Lifestyle (Fun, Enjoyment, Home Environment)

Rate Yourself	Outcome Goals
	1. 2. 3.

Wealth Notes

Step 2: Rate Yourself

On a scale of 0 to 10, rate how far (0) or close (10) you are to achieving your outcome goals in each area of life. Just flip back and drop your rating in the "Rate Yourself" column.

Step 3: Get Clear On Your Priorities

Look at where you're at in each area and reflect on what you want to prioritize in the next 30 days. Rank each one in order of priority — 1 being most important, 10 being least important.

Step 4: Determine Your Divine Desire

These big goals across your life are powerful and will make an impact. While you could scatter your energy, focus on the one area that, if you really locked in on it now, would make everything else easier or fall into place.

Once you know your Divine Desire, ask yourself: *Which area of life does it live in?*

WEALTH NOTES

Outcome Goal Clarity

- **Define it clearly.** Looking at the area of life that is your Divine Desire, what is the top outcome goal you want to focus on? Be as specific as possible.

- **Describe success.** How will you know you have it? Is it money in the bank, a number on the scale, or the way you feel?

- **Imagine it fully.** What will you see, hear, feel, and experience once you've reached it?

- **Take stock.** Where are you right now in relation to your desired outcome?

- **List your resources.** What personal strengths, tools, or support do you already have to help you bridge the gap?

- **Find expanders.** Do you know someone who has achieved what you want? What resources did they have to get there — and how might you apply those to your own journey?

- **Apply what you see.** How can you use these resources or strategies yourself?

- **Name your why.** Why is this goal so important to you? What will it make possible in your life?

- **Notice the ripple.** Who else will be affected by this change, and how will their lives improve?

Wealth Notes

PROCESS GOAL CLARITY

Process goals are the regular actions or habits you commit to that will help you hit your outcome goals.

They're the daily steps that turn your big vision into reality.

Write down a few process goals that will keep you on track toward your top outcome goal.

_____

_____

_____

_____

_____

_____

_____

_____

_____

_____

_____

_____

_____

_____

WEALTH NOTES

ALIGN WITH YOUR BIGGER VISION

Why haven't you achieved what you desire (yet)?

- Reflecting on your outcome goals for your divine desire, why do you think you haven't achieved them up to this point?

- What current thoughts, beliefs, feelings, habits, patterns, actions, or behaviors are getting in the way?

- Be honest: what fears come up? What are you afraid of if you were to hit these goals?

- What are you afraid of losing if you reach these goals?

- Which parts of the process or journey intimidate you the most?

- What are you afraid will happen if you DON'T hit your goals?

- What are you afraid will happen if you DO hit your goals?

- What has not having or creating these goals cost you so far?

Wealth Notes

TURN IT AROUND

Imagine all the **good stuff** that could happen when you follow through on your process goals and hit your outcome goals.

- List the positive things the process goals will create.

- List every amazing thing that becomes possible when you hit those outcome goals.

- How does your life change? How does it ripple out to others?

WEALTH NOTES

CREATE NEW NON-NEGOTIABLES

What are your non-negotiables for hitting your top outcome goal?

What are you committed to experiencing along the way — and how do you want to feel, not just when you arrive, but every step of the journey?

Who Do You Want to Be?

Before you chase any outcome, **ask yourself this:** Who do you want to be while creating it? How do you want to show up?

Get crystal clear on the version of you who owns their thoughts, feelings, actions, and energy, and knows limitless possibilities are always on the table.

Why is now the time to change?

Are you ready to commit to all of this now?

Wealth Notes

ELICIT YOUR MONEY STORY

The First Step: Eliciting Your Money Story

Questions to Think About:

- What are your current beliefs about money, and how do they trace back to your childhood experiences?

- When you think about money, what emotions come up? Where do you feel them in your body—stomach, throat, head, or heart?

- What do you believe about money right now? Where did those beliefs come from?

- How did your family talk about money when you were growing up?

Wealth Notes

ELICIT YOUR MONEY STORY...CONT.

- How do you really feel about spending money compared to saving it?

- What fears or worries pop up when you think about your finances?

- How has your money story shaped the choices you make and the opportunities you've had?

Digging into these questions will get you closer to the truth behind your money mindset.

WEALTH NOTES

CHANGING YOUR BELIEFS

What's one negative belief you have about wealth?

- What changes when you zoom out and see the bigger picture?

- If a fly on the wall watched how you think about that belief, what might it notice?

- How silly or surprising would your money belief look from its perspective?

- What if you challenge that belief?

Example of a challenged belief:

Belief: I'll never be financially secure.
Question: How do you know you'll never be financially secure?
Belief: Because I've always struggled with money.
Question: You've always struggled?
Belief: Yeah.
Question: Not even when you had a good month or got a raise?
Belief: Well, I guess there were a few times.

What if you change the wording of your belief and pay attention to your way of communicating? Avoid words like, can't, or never.

What happens if you add the word "yet"?

Wealth Notes

GREAT GOAL HEIST

We'll break down your full one-year goal soon, but if you're itching to dive in now, go for it. You've got the mindset. You've got the tools. No more stalling. Make your move.

1. **Define Your Dream:** Get crystal clear on what you want. Write it like it's already happening.
2. **Break It Down:** Use the SMART method. Make every step count.
3. **Set the Date:** Deadlines, not suggestions. Put them on your calendar and commit.
4. **Take Action:** Move daily. Small wins stack fast.
5. Reflect and Adjust: Check in, pivot if needed, and keep going.

You're not waiting for success. You're building it. Let's get to work.

Wealth Notes

SEVEN STEP SORCERY SYSTEM

1. **What money goal would you like to achieve?** Yep, the one you just thought of a second ago. Write it down.

What will you see, hear, and feel when you have it?

2. **Where are you now in relation to your desired outcome? Draw out all the details.**

3. **How will you know you have your goal/desire?**

4. **What will this outcome give you?**
What will this goal make possible for you? For what purpose do you want it?
   - What will this goal let you do or experience?
   - Why do you want it?
   - What will change in your life if you get it?
   - What might you lose or have to let go of to reach it?
   - Does this goal feel aligned with who you are and what matters to you?

-Are there drawbacks?

Wealth Notes

SEVEN STEP SORCERY SYSTEM...CONT.

5. Establish resources
- What personal resources do you have that will allow you to achieve this?
- Do you know anyone else who has achieved it? What resources did they have?

Close your eyes and imagine you already have it. Other than those mentioned, what resources did you use to get it?

6. Why now? Why did you choose that amount of money?

7. Put yourself in the future and write it in the present tense -
- **Pick a specific future date and put it down on paper.** "Next month" is too vague.
  - Write it like this: "It is now August 12th, 2026, and …"

- **Always write in the present tense: "I have..." "I am..." or "I do..."** (not "I will have" or "I will do").

State your outcome with positive language

Put it all together in a sentence: Example: It is now August 12th, 2026 and I have $_____…"

Wealth Notes

ADDITIONAL QUESTIONS TO TEST YOUR GOAL

"As you think about the goal you came up with…"

1. What will happen if you get it?
- How will your life look or feel different?
- What new opportunities will open up?
- What thoughts or feelings come up when you imagine it happening?

2. What will happen if you don't get it?
- What will stay the same if nothing changes?
- What challenges or frustrations will keep showing up?
- How will that impact you long-term?

3. What won't happen if you get it?
- What struggles or problems will disappear?
- What patterns will no longer control you

4. What won't happen if you don't get it?
- What possibilities will you miss out on?
- What experiences will you never have if you stay where you are?

Wrap-up instruction:

If these questions make your goal feel stronger and more aligned, keep going. If they weaken it or raise doubts, that's a sign to adjust your goal so it fully supports you.

Go back to Step 1 and refine it until it feels right.

Wealth Notes

Wealthy Magic Script

Create a gratitude/goal statement—what I call a Magic Script—that connects to the Seven Step Sorcery System you just applied. Write it in the **present tense** and in **positive language**, affirming your goal as if it's already true.

- Start with a longer version that lays out the foundation of everything you're calling in. Write it three times so you really feel it sink in.
- Then create a shorter version you can say or write often, so you stay connected to it daily.

Write your gratitude statement and say it out loud, DAILY.

Embody It Fully

Create an internal representation of your goal:
- *See what you'll see*
- *Hear what you'll hear*
- *Feel what you'll feel*
- *Taste what you'll taste*
- *Smell what you'll smell*

Step into that version of you. Notice your posture, your energy, your movement as you live it. Embody the mood and feeling of achieving the goal (e.g., confident, happy, excited).

Write both out, keep them where you can see them, and speak them daily.

Wealth Notes

YEARLY GOAL

1 Year Goal

Let's start with your 1-year goal. Write it down.

9 Month Goal

At nine months in, you'd be just three months away from hitting your goal. By then, your income would be stacking up toward that one year milestone.

Write your 9-month goal.

Now think back—how did you get there?

What choices, actions, and support made it possible?

Write how you got to your 9-month goal.

Wealth Notes

6 Month Goal

Where would you have to be in 6 months to set up your 9-month milestone?

Write your 6-month goal.

What helped you reach your 6-month goal?

What actions, learning, or support made it possible?

Write how you got to your 6-month goal.

3 Month Goal

Where would you have to be in 3 months to set up your 6-month milestone?

Write your 3-month goal.

What helped you reach your 3-month goal?

What actions, learning, or support made it possible?

Write how you got to your 3-month goal.

WEALTH NOTES

1 Month Goal

Where would you have to be in 1 months to set up your 3-month milestone?

Write your 1-month goal.

What helped you reach your 1-month goal? What actions, learning, or support made it possible?

Write how you got to your 1-month goal.

1 Week Goal

Once you have the one-month goal written, then ask, Where do you need to be a week from now in order to hit that 1 month goal?

Write your 1-week goal.

How did you achieve your 1-week goal?

Write how you achieved your 1-week goal.

Daily Goals

Then you can break it down DAILY. What are you committed to doing today (and every day for the rest of the week) to make sure this one-week goal becomes your reality?

Write today's goal and how you plan on making it happen!

Finish strong and commit fully today, and watch how those small daily wins stack up into unstoppable momentum.

Wealth Notes

SPENDING REALITY
VS
SPENDING FANTASY

Home

Investment	Current Amount	Desired Amount
Mortgage/rent payment		
Utilities		
Homeowner's insurance		
Repairs/Maintenance		
Decor		
Cleaning service		
Other:		
TOTAL:		

Transportation (Car, Bus, Taxi, Snow Machine, Boat)

Investment	Current Amount	Desired Amount
Payment(s)		
Insurance		
Fuel Repair/		
Maintenance		
Other:		
TOTAL:		

Wealth Notes

Health + Wellness

Investment	Current Amount	Desired Amount
Groceries		
Eating out		
Ordering in		
Coffee		
Gym membership		
Private chef		
Other:		
TOTAL:		

Fun + Self-Care

Investment	Current Amount	Desired Amount
Travel		
Gifts		
Clothes		
Mani/Pedi/Facial		
Massages/Spas		
Yoga		
Other:		
TOTAL:		

Wealth Notes

Children (and/or pets)

Investment	Current Amount	Desired Amount
Daycare		
Clothes		
Healthcare		
Food/Supplements		
Toys		
Schools/Activities		
Other:		
TOTAL:		

Payments

Investment	Current Amount	Desired Amount
Credit card payments		
Student loans		
Personal loans		
Other:		
TOTAL:		

Wealth Notes

Business Investments

Investment	Current Amount	Desired Amount
Coaches/Teachers/Trainer		
Courses/Memberships		
Travel		
Team/Employees		
Client gifts		
Marketing/Advertisement		
Software		
Other:		
TOTAL:		

Miscellaneous

Investment	Current Amount	Desired Amount
Charities/Donations		
Savings account		
Taxes		
Retirement		
Life insurance		
Bank fees		
Other:		
TOTAL:		

WEALTH NOTES

CRAFTING A DAY OF INTENTION

My mornings are sacred, built around rituals that align with how I feel and what I need to start the day strong. These practices vary, sometimes focusing on just one or blending several to match my mood. Here's a glimpse of some AM rituals:

- Breathwork
- Reading
- Journaling
- Writing content
- Pulling tarot cards
- Meditation/Visualization
- Listening to podcasts
- Running
- Walking my dogs
- Being in nature
- Yoga/Stretching
- EFT (Tapping)
- Affirmations
- Daily Incantation: 3 powerful statements each morning to set your tone for the day.

(Sometimes I do just one of these things, a mix, or all, depending on how I'm feeling.)

What morning rituals do you want to add to your routine that could shape who you are and push you closer to success?

Wealth Notes

ENDING THE DAY WITH INTENTION

Just like mornings kick off fresh starts, evenings are your time to slow down and reset. PM rituals help you separate the chaos of the day from the calm you need. These are some that supported me the most when life felt heavy:

- Log out of social media
- Play music and light a candle
- Go for a walk
- Yoga
- Make and enjoy a nourishing meal
- Connect with your partner
- Read
- Bath with essential oils
- Journaling/Affirmations
- Personal development reading
- Meditate

Wrap up by reflecting on your day, whether or not anything big happened. Processing and releasing the day is powerful—it clears space and resets you, just like we do with the wins and lessons in our money journey.

What evening rituals could you add to bring more calm and purpose to your nights?

Wealth Notes

Craft Your Affirmations

Take a moment to write down some custom affirmations that reflect the wealthy version of you. Start each one with 'I am' or 'I choose.' Focus on statements that feel true or that you want to become true, like 'I am worthy of wealth,' 'I choose to see opportunities everywhere,' or 'I am building financial freedom daily.'

Now, write your own affirmations in the space provided.

_____

_____

_____

_____

_____

_____

_____

_____

_____

_____

_____

_____

Wealth Notes

What Makes Your Heart Tingle

We're going after EXACTLY what you would do in a perfect world. Grab a pen and a piece of paper...

- **Write ALL the things you love to do, BIG or SMALL.**

- **Write ALL the things you do not enjoy doing, BIG or SMALL.**

Take a minute and picture yourself waking up in that life, your ideal one. Coffee in hand, maybe you're meditating, doing yoga, or just sitting in peace. Walk yourself through your day.

1. What's your routine?
2. How long are your workdays?
3. Who are you spending time with?

Make it vivid. Make it real.

See what you're going to see, hear what you're going to hear, and really feel all the feelings you will be feeling.

WEALTH NOTES

WEEKLY RITUALS: LOCK IT IN

Pick one weekly ritual that keeps you locked into your vision.

Start by letting go of doubts and limiting beliefs. No judgment, just release. As the week goes on, old patterns might try to sneak back in. Notice them, call them out for what they are, just old stories, and let them go.

Habits are automatic. They're the unconscious, repeated actions you do without thinking, like brushing your teeth, scrolling your phone first thing in the morning, or pouring coffee as soon as you wake up.

Rituals are intentional. They're habits with meaning attached. You do them on purpose, with awareness, to set energy, mindset, or identity. Journaling in the morning, lighting a candle before work, or repeating affirmations are rituals because they carry significance and intention.

Put simply: **A habit is what you do. A ritual is how and why you do it.**

Now, pick one weekly ritual that keeps you locked into your vision. Write it all out in detail and start that ritual today!

WEALTH NOTES

Wealth Notes

Wealth Notes

Wealth Notes

A

Attract

Where your thoughts, feelings, and actions align with your desires. Alignment pulls wealth your way.

5-Minute Future Self Embodiment

This one's fast but potent. Choose a time of day when you can commit to five focused minutes. No distractions. Sit still, close your eyes, and see your future self living the life you're calling in. Imagine them walking through their day.

- *How do they move?*
- *How do they talk?*
- *What do they wear?*
- *What do they say yes to?*
- *How do they respond to stress, to success, to everyday decisions?*

Now here's where most people stop, but you're not most people. Don't just watch. Step into them. Be them. Embody their energy in your breath, your posture, your face, your voice. What does confidence feel like in your body? What does wealth feel like in your skin? Stay in that version of you for the full five minutes.

This daily five-minute practice begins to hardwire your nervous system for the version of you that already has it all. Repetition creates identity. Identity creates action. Action creates results. You're not trying to get there—you're already there. This isn't about fantasy, it's about frequency. This is about giving your body a new normal. Your brain learns through experience, not theory, and this is you teaching it who you really are.

If you skip a day, fine. Start again the next. But keep showing up. When you do, the world starts to shift around you.

Wealth Notes

NIGHTLY PLAYBACK

Right before bed is when your subconscious is wide open. What you think about in that window stays with you longer and sinks deeper. You've spent all day in your current reality. But you don't have to go to sleep in it.

Replay the day as if it went exactly how your highest self would've lived it. Imagine yourself making bold moves, hearing yes, hitting the goals, feeling clear, grounded, focused, and powerful. Did you say something you wish you hadn't? *Rewrite it.* Did you hold back on something? Picture yourself going for it instead. Your brain can't tell the difference, so give it the version you actually want.

Your brain can't tell the difference between real and vividly imagined experiences. Neuroscience shows it fires the same way either way. Brain scans show that the same areas light up whether you're doing the thing or imagining it. It also doesn't process negatives well. So if you say, 'I hate debt,' or 'I have so much debt,' your brain zeroes in on the word debt and reinforces that image. This is why it's so important to picture and phrase what you do want, not what you don't.

Replay it all—how you walked, how you spoke, what results came in. Feel the emotion of that ideal day in your body. Then carry that into sleep. That version of your day becomes the blueprint your mind holds onto through the night.

This isn't pretending things didn't happen. It's overriding what you don't want to keep replaying. The world already replays your limitations every time you open your phone or scroll social media. This is about shifting the story back in your favor. **Take that five-minute window before bed and own it.** Your future is shaped by what your mind rehearses. Train it wisely.

Wealth Notes

MIRROR EMBODIMENT WORK

Stand in front of a mirror. Look yourself in the eyes. Now speak. Not like a robot. Speak like you mean it—with energy, emotion, and certainty. Tell yourself who you are. Who you're becoming. What you're calling in. Say it until your voice matches the vision. Say it until your body believes it. Even if your brain resists, keep going.

Say things like:
- "I've got this."
- "I make shit happen."
- "Money flows to me."
- "I'm not backing down."
- "I'm stronger than my excuses."
- "I trust myself."
- "I win."
- "I move with confidence."
- "I keep going."
- "I create results."
- "I'm already the version of me I'm stepping into."

This isn't about convincing yourself. It's about claiming it. Most people speak more truth to strangers than they do to themselves, but this changes that. When your subconscious hears you say it out loud with belief behind it, it registers it as real. You're rewiring the program, rewriting the script, and replacing the old junk with a new direction.

Try this for two minutes a day. Set a timer if you need to. Morning is great, but any time works. You don't need to feel "on" or supercharged; you just need to show up. Your voice carries power, and when you turn that power inward, that's when you start leading your life instead of just reacting to it.

Wealth Notes

POWER ANCHOR

Choose one physical object to represent your future self.

It could be a bracelet, a necklace, a rock, or a keychain. The object itself doesn't matter. What matters is what it reminds you of.

Just like a song or a smell can instantly trigger a memory, your chosen object can trigger the feelings of wealth, confidence, or success you're stepping into. Every time you see it or touch it, take a few seconds to drop into that version of you.

The more you connect this object with your chosen identity, the stronger the anchor becomes. Over time, it becomes your reminder and your reset button back to power.

On the next page, write down:

- *The object you've chosen as your anchor*
- *The emotion or identity you're attaching to it*
- *Why you chose it*

Wealth Notes

CURRENT REALITY VS DESIRED REALITY

Answer the following as honestly as you can:

Go through these questions and write your current reality in the left column, and then go back through and write your desired reality (aka if anything were possible, and you were living your best version of life) in the right column.

What is the first thing you do when you wake up in the morning?

Current Reality	Desired Reality

What does your morning ritual/routine look like?

Current Reality	Desired Reality

What do you wear at home, and how do you feel in those clothes?

Current Reality	Desired Reality

WEALTH NOTES

What do you wear when you go out with friends, and how do you feel in those clothes?

Current Reality	Desired Reality

What kinds of food do you eat, and how do they make you feel?

Current Reality	Desired Reality

Where do you usually eat your meals? At your desk, kitchen table, or couch? Or are meals one of those things you forget exist half the time?

Current Reality	Desired Reality

What type of exercise (if any) do you do, and how does it make you feel?

Current Reality	Desired Reality

How do you usually spend your free time?

Current Reality	Desired Reality

Wealth Notes

What does your home look like?

Current Reality	Desired Reality

How does your home environment feel like?

Current Reality	Desired Reality

How do you practice self-care, and how often?

Current Reality	Desired Reality

What role does spirituality play in your everyday life?

Current Reality	Desired Reality

What support systems do you have in your life?

Current Reality	Desired Reality

WEALTH NOTES

Look at your "Current Reality" vs. your "Desired Reality" and answer the following questions:

- How close are they? Are they almost aligned, or miles apart?
- What do you feel is standing in the way of your dream life?
- What's one small step you can take for each area that moves you closer to that desired life?

Create an Action Plan

An action plan breaks your big goals into short-term steps that move you closer to what you want. The smaller tasks add up and lead you to the bigger outcome.

Ask yourself:

- What will I do between now and next week?
- How will I finish the task at hand?
- What's the final step I need to reach this goal? (Work backwards.)
- What do I need to do differently this time to actually get results?
- What don't I want to do but know I must?

Let's get real about Divine Desires. This isn't some soft concept. It's built from the gritty, beautiful moments that shape who we are.

Wealth Notes

4D Exercise

Spot Your Dreams
Start by getting really clear on your bigger vision. Write down all the details of what you want—your dreams and desires. As you do this, notice any "yeah, but" thoughts that sneak in. Write those doubts down too.
Example: "I want to own my own home." Then the doubt shows up: "But I don't know if I can afford it." Write it down.

Catch the Doubts
Say your dreams and desires out loud, one by one. Pay attention to any negative thoughts that rise up. Write those down.
Example: "I save money every month." Then your brain chimes in: "It won't be enough." Or, "I don't deserve this." Or, "I'm not capable."

Flip the Dead Ends
Look at the doubts you wrote. Where did they come from? When did you start believing them? Are they actually true? Challenge them. Question them. Decide if they've earned a place in your life—or if they're just blocking your way forward.

Return to Your Desires
Circle back to what you really want. Say out loud what you're choosing to believe now. Put your eyes on where you're going, not the doubts you've already exposed.

Wealth Notes

INJECTING FUN AND WEALTH INTO EVERYDAY LIFE

Here's what I want you to do:

- Change your alert tones to sound like money.

- Switch up your passwords so they're little mantras in disguise.

- Keep your eyes peeled for repeating numbers—111, 444, 888.

- Rename your bank accounts so they match your goals. Call it "Freedom Fund," "Adventure Account," or "Wealth Well."

- Give your wallet a makeover. Your wallet should feel like a space wealth would want to live in.

The truth is, we make money hard. We overthink it, stress over it, obsess about how it's going to come.

But when we ease into the idea that money is everywhere, that it's trying to show up for us in big and small ways—we shift.

Our mindset shifts. Our energy shifts. And suddenly, we're open. Let this be your starting point. Make this fun. Let it be easy.

Because money doesn't just come when we hustle—it comes when we align.

WEALTH NOTES

GRATITUDE SEALS THE DEAL

Merriam-Webster defines Gratitude as *"the state of being grateful; thankfulness."*

But gratitude is more than a polite thank you. It's a choice. It's noticing the good even when life feels heavy and choosing to center on what's working instead of spiraling about what's not.

Say it clearly and don't water it down.

Gratitude has power. It shifts your energy fast and raises your frequency, whether you're having a good day or not. What you focus on multiplies. When you start leading with appreciation, life responds with more to appreciate. But if you brush it off or stop noticing the good, don't be shocked when it dries up.

Gratitude is simple, but its ripple effect is massive.

Now it's your turn to move.

Choose one act of generosity that means something to you.

Not for show.
Not for a gold star or a smelly sticker.
Do it because it feels right and reflects who you are.
That kind of giving sends a loud signal to the universe.
It says you're in.
You trust there's enough.
And you're ready for more.

Gratitude isn't a personality trait. It's a practice.

Wealth Notes

GRATITUDE LIST

Make a list of 25 things you're grateful for right now. Sit down, breathe deep, and actually feel it.

Start with the everyday stuff you overlook—your breath, your body, the roof over your head, the food in your kitchen.

Wealth Notes

GRATITDUE LIST STRETCHED

Then stretch it. Be grateful for the smell of fresh coffee, the sound of crickets at night, the sidewalk that carries you home, the way music shifts your mood, even the smell of rain on pavement. Random or obvious, big or small—it all counts.

Here's a simple way to play with it:

- Write down 5 things you can see right now.

- Write down 5 things you can hear.

- Write down 5 things you can touch or feel.

- Write down 5 things you can smell or taste.

- Write down 5 people, memories, or opportunities that make your life better.

By the time you get halfway, you'll notice the shift. Your energy, your focus, even your mood starts to change. That's the power of actually feeling it, not just writing it down.

Don't just practice gratitude when things are going well. Make it part of who you are.

WEALTH NOTES

Aligning with the Frequency of Money

Step 1: Reflect and Write
Take a few minutes to reflect on your current money beliefs. What do you honestly believe about money right now? Write them down. List both the positive and the negative, even the ones that feel small or silly. If you need a refresher, go back to the chapter on beliefs and pull from there.

Step 2: Evaluate and Challenge
Look at each belief and ask yourself, "Is this helping me attract wealth, or is it holding me back?" For the negative ones, dig deeper. Ask, *"Where did this come from? Is it even mine, or did I pick it up from someone else?"*

Step 3: Transform and Affirm
Take every limiting belief and flip it into one that supports the wealthy life you are building. *Example: "Money is hard to come by"* becomes *"Money flows to me easily and often."*

Step 4: Imagine Abundance
Close your eyes and play the wealth movie in your mind. See your bank account rising. Watch your debts get wiped out. Imagine opportunities showing up like clockwork. Feel the emotions of that version of you—joy, safety, gratitude—and lock them in. That is the frequency.

Step 5: Lock in a Money Mindset
Pick one strong affirmation and make it yours. *Example: "I am a magnet for financial abundance and aligned opportunities."*

Say it every morning, every night, and anytime your thoughts start spiraling. Then write down three money wins from your day, no matter how small.

Wealth Notes

SOCIAL CURRENCY

Purpose: Gauge your current social currency and find ways to boost your wealth in relationships and connections.
Instructions:

1. List Your Networks
Write down all your social and professional networks—online (LinkedIn, Instagram, Facebook, TikTok) and in-person (clubs, groups, communities).

2. Evaluate Your Engagement
Rate your activity in each network from 1 (low) to 10 (high).
Think about the value you give and the value you get from these groups/platforms.

3. Identify Key Relationships
Pick out key people who impact your social currency—mentors, peers, influencers. *Note why these relationships matter and how they add to your wealth.*

4. Action Plan
Choose at least two networks or relationships to engage with more.
Set clear goals like starting a project, offering help, or sharing resources.

5. Reflection
At the end of the month, check in with yourself. Notice any new opportunities, connections, or insights that came from showing up more.

This will give you a clear view of your social currency and steps to grow it, boosting your overall wealth.

Wealth Notes

THE 2.0 SWITCH

Step 1: Spot the Old Self: Write down the qualities of your current identity that no longer work for you.
Example: "I'm inconsistent. I doubt myself. I avoid responsibility. I'm passive when it comes to opportunities."

Step 2: Claim Your 2.0 Qualities: Choose three to five qualities your next-level self embodies fully.
Example: "I am disciplined. I am reliable. I am resourceful. I am ambitious. I am confident with money."

Step 3: Anchor It Physically: Close your eyes, breathe deep, and imagine yourself stepping into a room where your 2.0 self already lives. Notice how they walk, how they hold themselves, and what they're wearing. Do they look polished, relaxed, powerful? Picture their posture, their expression, their energy. Feel the confidence, calm, or excitement they carry. Step into that version of you in your mind, take a breath, and lock it in.

Step 4: Act It Out Today: Pick one small action your 2.0 self would do today and actually do it. Maybe it's checking your account without fear. Maybe it's finally making that phone call you've been putting off. Maybe it's choosing a healthier meal instead of defaulting to old habits. Every action reinforces the switch.

Step 5: Repeat and Reinforce: Every morning ask yourself, "Am I acting from my old self or my 2.0 self?" Keep choosing 2.0. Over time, it becomes automatic.

When you make the 2.0 Switch, the people around you feel it too. Your upgraded self shows up differently in every relationship, every opportunity, and every decision.

Wealth Notes

DIRECT IMPACT EXERCISE

1. Revisit Your List
Pull out the list you wrote earlier of people who would be directly impacted by your wealth.

2. Add Details
Don't just write "my parents" or "my kids." Write what would actually change. Would your parents travel more? Would your kids have more opportunities? Would your employees feel more secure? Spell it out.

3. Expand the Ripple
Think beyond the obvious. Who else gets lifted when you rise? A neighbor? A community? A cause?

4. Visualize the Shift
Close your eyes and walk through the scenarios. Picture your success unfolding in real time. What does it look like? What does it feel like?

5. Anchor the Emotion
Notice the gratitude, relief, joy, and pride that ripple through these moments. Lock those emotions in. That feeling is fuel.

Now it's time to go beyond the list and see what it looks like when those changes are real. Don't just think about who benefits, imagine the scenes playing out as if they're happening right now.

Write three specific scenes your wealth would create.

Choose one scene and name the first action you will take this week, whether that means making a call, setting a transfer, introducing a connection, or putting a date on the calendar.

WEALTH NOTES

Wealth Notes

WEALTH NOTES

WEALTH NOTES

L

Language

The words you use shape how you see yourself, your wealth, and what is possible for you.

IDENTIFY. QUESTION. REWRITE.

Top 5 Signs You're Operating from a Limiting Belief:

- You hesitate on opportunities you actually want
- You downplay your wins or brush off compliments
- You keep sabotaging progress just when things start going well
- You repeat the same patterns with money, love, or health
- Your inner voice is a full-time hater, not a coach

Also Words like:
"I always attract the wrong people."
"I'll never lose the weight."
"I'm not smart enough to succeed."
"I'm just not cut out for more."

Your beliefs are just thoughts you've repeated so many times they feel like facts, but they're not. They're learned patterns, and you have the power to change them.

1. **Spot the behavior that keeps looping,** like overspending, procrastinating, or ghosting your own goals.
2. **Identify the belief driving it.** For example: "I'm not smart enough" or "People like me don't succeed."
3. **Trace it back.** Where did you pick it up — childhood, a breakup, an old job?
4. **Question it.** Is this even true? Is it your truth, or something you inherited?
5. **Replace it.** Choose a belief that actually supports you. Say it. Own it. Live it.

Wealth Notes

Squash Any Limiting Belief

What's one limiting belief you're ready to let go of today? Here's how to shift it, especially around money:

1. **Identify the behavior.** What keeps showing up? Are you procrastinating, overspending, or ghosting your own goals?
2. **Pinpoint the belief.** What thought or assumption is feeding that behavior? What belief keeps giving it permission to exist?
3. **Trace it back to the root.** Where did it start? Childhood, a breakup, a job, or something you were told?
4. **Ask why you've held onto it.** What role has it played? Did it protect you or give you certainty?
5. **Name what it costs you.** What has this belief taken from you? How much emotionally, financially, or in your growth? What is the real price of keeping it?
6. **Question the truth.** Is it fact, or just a story you have repeated too many times?
7. **Create a new belief.** Choose one that supports who you are becoming.
8. **Anchor it daily.** Act like it is already true. Your subconscious does not care if it is imagined or real, it will respond either way.

It all starts with what you believe is possible. So, what do you want to believe from this point forward? You get to decide. Right here. Right now.

Wealth Notes

MONEY ANGLE

Money is neutral. But your beliefs about it? Those are loaded. They come from childhood, media, religion, culture, and trauma. And they can block your wealth more than anything else.

Ask yourself:
- What did I hear about money growing up?
- What did I see my caregivers do with money?
- How do I talk about money now?

Are you saying things like:
- "Money doesn't grow on trees."
- "We can't afford that."
- "People with money are selfish."
- "I'm not good with money."

Those aren't facts. They're beliefs. And they're shaping your financial reality right now.

To shift them:
- Start talking about money in a positive way.
- Practice gratitude for what you have.
- Visualize wealth as safe, expansive, and aligned.
- Learn to manage money with joy, not dread.

Your net worth will rarely grow beyond your self-worth. That isn't just a nice phrase, it's the foundation.

Stop waiting for perfection, permission, or proof. Ditch the scripts you didn't write. Start telling stories that fit who you're becoming. You were never meant to live in a box someone else built. You *were* made for more. It's time to start believing it.

Wealth Notes

LAYERS OF BELIEF

Everything you believe has layers and when we peel back the layers and rebuild, we reach our core. The goal is to move past the surface noise and get to the root. That's where the healing happens.

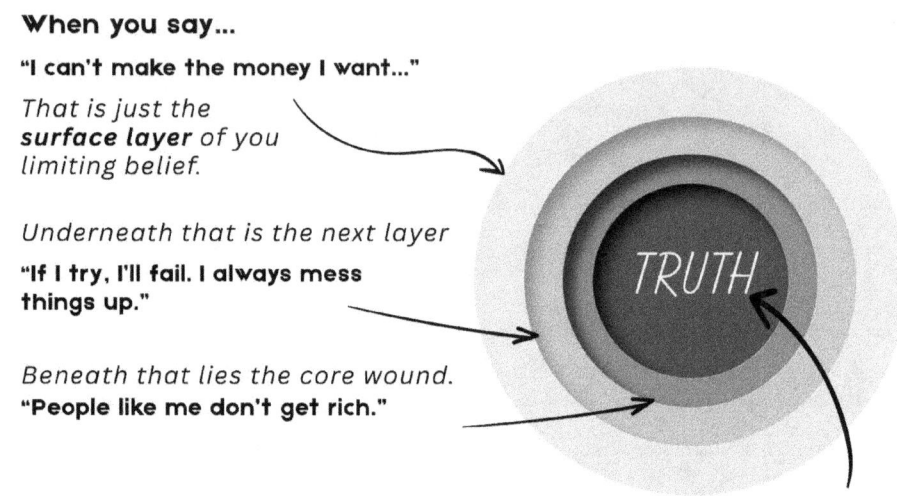

When you say...
"I can't make the money I want..."

*That is just the **surface layer** of you limiting belief.*

Underneath that is the next layer
"If I try, I'll fail. I always mess things up."

Beneath that lies the core wound.
"People like me don't get rich."

THE TRUTH = "I create wealth because I'm meant for more."

Sometimes just seeing it clearly is enough to shake something loose. Awareness opens the door. The work starts there.

Start with the surface belief, peel back the next layers, then land at the core:

- What's the belief on the surface?
- What's underneath that?
- Is there another layer?
- What's the foundational root belief that, when shifted, changes the rest?

WEALTH NOTES

Belief Bridging: Rewiring What You Believe

We walk ourselves across the bridge one plank at a time.

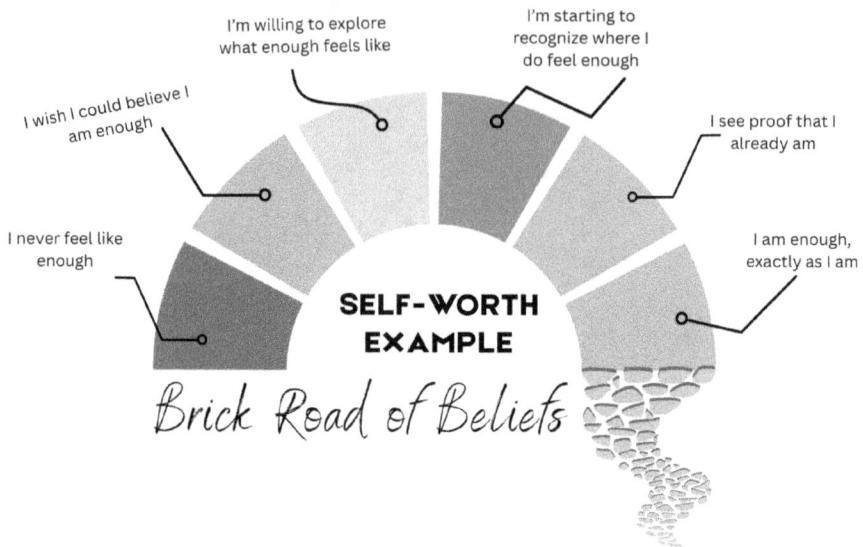

Start with your Brick Road of Beliefs. Write them out step by step:

1. What's the belief you're carrying right now that weighs you down? (Brick 1)
2. What's the belief you actually want to hold — the truth your Wealthy Self has always known? (Brick 6)
3. What's your Belief Bridge — the steps in between that feel believable enough to move you closer, one brick at a time? (Bricks 2–5)

Wealth Notes

Belief Bridging: Rewiring What You Believe...cont.

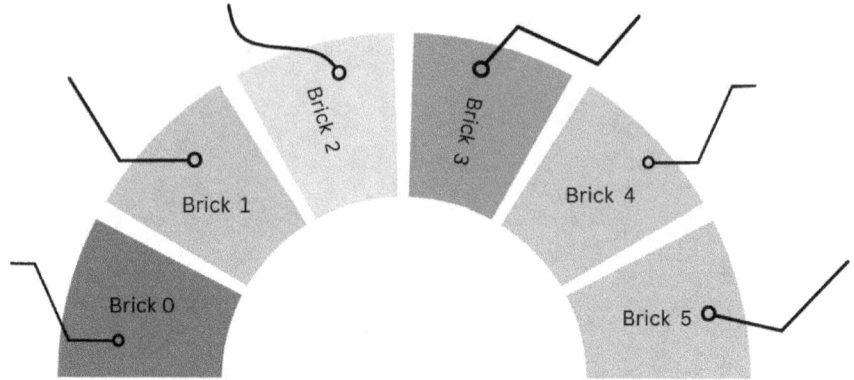

Use this space around each block to jot down your shifting beliefs, or recreate your own Brick Road on a separate piece of paper.

Stuck? Use this Brick 1–6 checklist

1. **Brick 1:** Name the current belief holding you back.
2. **Brick 2:** I want to believe _____.
3. **Brick 3:** I am open to _____.
4. **Brick 4:** I can imagine myself believing _____.
5. **Brick 5:** I can find proof I am starting to live _____.
6. **Brick 6:** New truth I choose now: _____.

Each brick you lay down is a new rule.

What do you want to be true? What would feel good, even if it sounds like a stretch right now? Try these:
- The more I enjoy my life, the more money flows in
- Opportunities show up for me in surprising ways
- Money comes to me in both expected and unexpected streams
- The more I trust myself, the more abundance grows
- Rest, fun, and joy fuel my wealth

These are your rules now. Make them real and speak them out loud. Believe them and live by them.

Wealth Notes

SCRIPTED SPELLS

Here's a simple exercise to start catching and shifting your everyday thoughts.

1. **Become aware of your thoughts.** Notice what keeps coming up during the day.
2. **Record your thoughts.** Write down what's running through your mind, the good and the bad.
3. **Evaluate your thoughts.** Ask yourself if each thought brings you closer to or farther from your goals. If it brings you closer, keep it. If not, move to the next step.
4. **Shift to empowering thoughts.** Rewrite the negative ones into stronger statements.
   Examples:
   - "In the past, I used to believe _____. Now I'm learning how to _____."
   - "The truth is _____."
   - "I'm open to the idea that _____ is possible."
   - "I can see how _____ could become my reality."
   - If you're wrestling with feelings of inadequacy, like "I don't know enough," flip it to something more constructive:
   - *"I've been soaking up knowledge through books, resources, and courses for 3 years. I know a lot and I'm learning to rewire my brain for success."*

5. **Track and notice.** Notice the ones that keep showing up. Those repeats are your patterns, and once you see them, you can change them.

Do it for a week and it starts to feel automatic. The results make it worth it.

WEALTH NOTES

MONEY INCANTATIONS

Here are some sample money incantations for you to consider. You're encouraged to tailor them to your liking or create your own in the space provided.

- I effortlessly achieve every goal I set.
- I feel powerful, smart, and courageous.
- Wealth and abundance fill my life.
- Abundance is my natural state.
- Money flows to me easily, frequently, and abundantly.
- I am worthy of wealth and abundance.
- I am open to receiving more money and success.
- Creative ideas for wealth and success flow from me.
- I see abundance and opportunity everywhere.
- My income is constantly increasing.
- Money flows quickly to me from unexpected sources.
- I attract financial prosperity into every aspect of my life.
- I am unstoppable, courageous, and powerful.
- I always have enough money for anything I want.

Every time you say one, you're retraining your mind to expect wealth, not just wishing for it. Let them run through your head like your favorite playlist. Say them in the mirror, shout them in your car, write them in your journal.

Wealth Notes

Own It With 'I Am'

The most powerful words in the English language combined is **I AM.** Whatever comes after it? That's your identity. That's your direction. The "I am" statement is no joke—it's the blueprint your subconscious builds from.

Who do you need to become to live the life you know is yours?

Speak it into existence:

I am powerful.
I am confident.
I am magnetic.
I am a beam of light.
I am intelligent.
I am a force of good.
I am creative.
I am valuable.
I am successful.
I am beautiful.
I am loved.

These aren't just words. This is identity work.

Now it's your turn. Write it. Repeat it. Feel it.

I am...
I am...
I am...
I am...
I am...

Put it on Post-it notes. In your affirmations app. On your lock screen. On a card in your wallet. Keep it in your face, in your energy, in your subconscious.

Write it out.

Wealth Notes

REFLECT & APPLY THE UNIVERSAL LAWS

Manifestation: The phenomenon that occurs when something that was originally a part of your imagination becomes actualized into your physical reality.

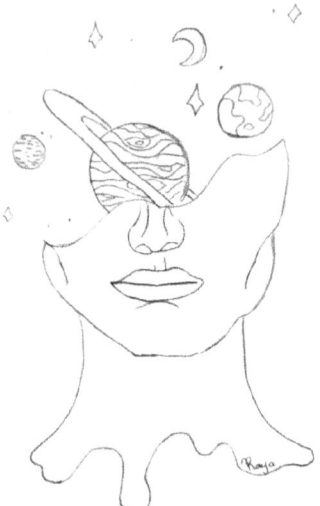

My daughter was 12-years-old when she came home from school and said:
"Mom, I don't know if anyone's ever taken a picture of the mind, so I drew one for you."
Children are always listening, absorbing information, consciously and unconsciously!

1. Which universal law hits home for you the most?

2. How can you see yourself using this law in your daily life right now?

3. What shifted in the way you look at wealth, success, or alignment after reading this chapter?

4. When you think about your next big move, which law do you want guiding you?

5. What does living in alignment with the universal laws mean to you personally?

Use this to anchor what you've learned. Don't just read the laws, decide how you'll live them.

Wealth Notes

Laws at a Glance Cheat Sheet

Quick, badass one-liners for each law:

- **Law of Oneness:** We're all connected.
- **Law of Vibration:** Match the mood of what you want.
- **Law of Action:** Manifestation needs movement. Get off your butt.
- **Law of Correspondence:** Inner world = outer world.
- **Law of Cause and Effect:** You reap what you plant. Karma, baby.
- **Law of Attraction:** Like attracts like.
- **Law of Transmutation:** High vibe eats low vibe for breakfast. Shift energy. Alchemize it.
- **Law of Compensation:** Give + receive. Period.
- **Law of Relativity:** Your problems aren't permanent.
- **Law of Polarity:** Contrast creates clarity.
- **Law of Gender:** Balance your hustle with flow.
- **Law of Rhythm:** Everything moves in cycles. Find your flow.

Wealth Notes

Wealth Notes

Wealth Notes

Wealth Notes

T
Thought-catching

The practice of noticing and shifting the thoughts that run on autopilot so you can choose wealth instead.

LET'S FLIP THE SCRIPT

1. Catch your thoughts

Pay attention to the chatter in your head. Notice all of it.

2. Write them down

The good, the bad, the annoying. Get it out of your head and onto paper.

3. Call them out

Ask yourself if this thought is helping you move forward or just keeping you stuck.

4. Rewire it

If it's trash, replace it with something that serves you. Use these prompts:

"In the past, I used to believe _____. Now, I'm learning to _____."
"The truth is _____."
"I'm open to the idea that _____ is possible."
"I can see how _____ could become real for me."

Example:

Instead of saying, "I don't know enough," flip it to, "I've been soaking up personal development for three years. I know a lot, and I'm learning how to turn it into real results."

5. Track the patterns

Tally the thoughts that keep repeating. Spot the loop and call it out.

Wealth Notes

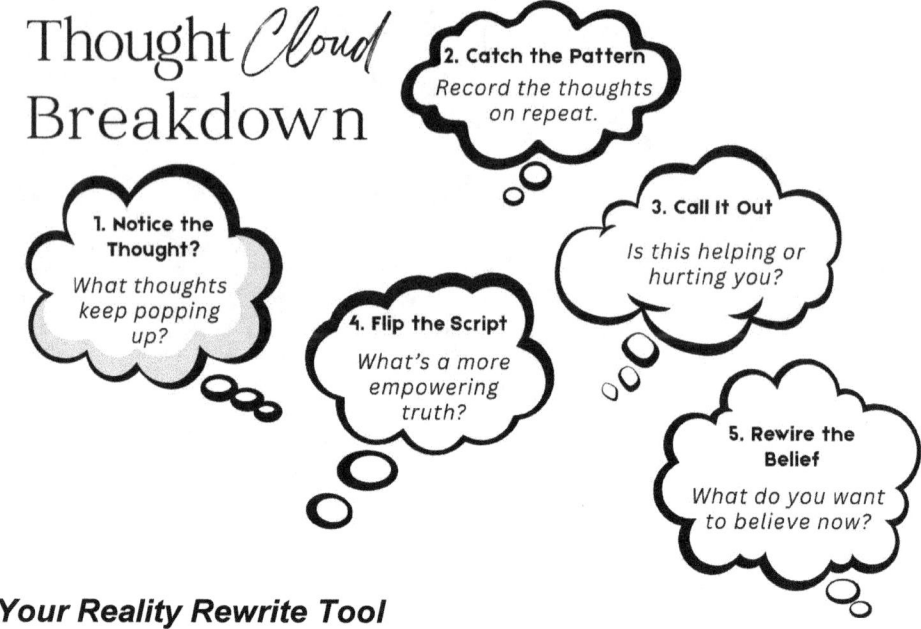

Your Reality Rewrite Tool

1. What thoughts keep popping up?

Write down three repeating thoughts that are not helping you.

2. Is this thought helping or hurting?

Next to each one, label it as helping or hurting.

3. What's the truth?

Flip the thought into something empowering.

Example: *"I'll never get out of debt" becomes "I'm learning how to manage money and build wealth."*

4. What do you want to believe instead?

Use one of these sentence starters to rewire it:

- "In the past, I used to believe... now I know..."
- "The truth is..."
- "I'm open to the idea that..."
- "It's possible that..."
- "I am becoming someone who..."

5. Track it daily for 7 days

Write your thought down each time it shows up. Use tally marks beside it so you can see how often it repeats. Then, right next to it, write a new version that helps you.

Wealth Notes

Spot Your Setpoint

Spot Your Setpoint
Track your capacity meter across all 8 life areas

Money
- What's the highest monthly income you've ever had?
- What happened right after?
- What's the number that usually triggers hustle or panic?

Career or Business
- What was your boldest move or biggest win?
- When did you start playing small again?
- What patterns keep repeating at the next level?

Health + Body
- What's your feel-good weight or energy level?
- When do your healthy habits fall off?
- What always pulls you back to your 'normal'?

Love + Relationships
- When has a relationship felt next-level?
- What triggered the disconnect or drama after that?
- Do you notice a cap on how good you let love get?

...cont

Wealth Notes

Friendships + Community
- When did you feel fully seen and supported?
- Did you pull back or isolate afterward?
- How many close connections do you truly let in?

Time + Freedom
- When did you feel the most free and spacious?
- What made you stop giving yourself that freedom?
- What patterns always steal your time back?

Self-Worth + Confidence
- When were you showing up unapologetically?
- What caused you to shrink again?
- What triggers doubt even when you're winning?

Joy + Fun
- What's the most lit-up you've felt recently?
- When did you stop letting yourself enjoy it?
- Do you feel guilty when life gets too good?

Now look at your setpoint across these areas.

What do your high points have in common? What tends to happen right after things feel really good?

Notice if your subconscious is trying to protect you from something. *That awareness shows you where the old pattern lives. Then shift into identity.*

Who do you need to become to live consistently at your next level? What beliefs, behaviors, and boundaries does that version of you hold? And what are you no longer available for? This is where you raise the bar on what you allow in your life and reset your baseline for good.

Wealth Notes

YOUR Capacity METER
IN ACTION

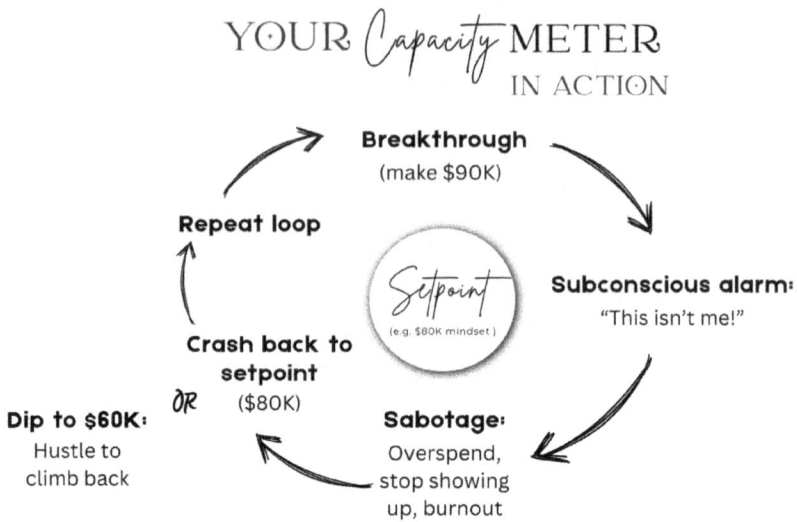

REPEAT LOOP - UNLESS IDENTITY SHFITS

Use the prompts below to track it for the next week:

Daily Check-In
- Where's my energy today on a scale from 1–10?
- Where's my money confidence today on a scale from 1–10?
- Did I notice myself holding back, avoiding, or sabotaging?

When Things Felt "Too Good"
- What happened right before I felt the urge to pull back?
- What thoughts showed up? (Example: "This won't last" or "I don't deserve this.")
- How did my body react? (Tension, fatigue, distraction, spending, overeating, etc.)

When Things Felt "Too Low"
- What triggered the drop?
- What behaviors kicked in? (Overworking, people-pleasing, shutting down, overspending, etc.)
- What signal told me I had to hustle harder or snap out of it?

Patterns
- Do I notice the same triggers or habits at both ends of the meter?
- How do I usually bring myself back to "normal"?
- What would it look like to hold steady at a slightly higher baseline?

Wealth Notes

Top 25 Limiting Beliefs

1. I'm not smart enough.
2. I'm not worthy of success.
3. I'm not good with money.
4. I always mess things up.
5. I have to work hard to make money.
6. I'll never get ahead.
7. I don't have what it takes.
8. If I shine too bright, I'll make others uncomfortable.
9. If people really knew me, they wouldn't like me.
10. I'm too old to start over.
11. It's selfish to want more.
12. People like me don't get rich.
13. I have to be perfect to succeed.
14. I don't have the time.
15. I've already missed my chance.
16. It's better to play it safe.
17. If I try, I'll probably fail, anyway.
18. I should just be grateful for what I have.
19. I'm too much.
20. It's too late for me.
21. Nothing I do is good enough.
22. What I have to say doesn't matter.
23. No one else has ever done it, so I can't.
24. Change is hard and takes forever.
25. I've tried before and it didn't work, so why bother?

WEALTH NOTES

MINDSHIFT MAGIC RECIPE

Ingredients:

1 cup Courage
2 tbsp Imagination
A pinch of Self-Reflection
A dash of Creativity
A sprinkle of Dreams

Instructions:
Light a candle. Get cozy. Breathe deep.
Ask yourself: *What rules or non-negotiables have you created for your life?* Write every belief that pops up. Do not filter your answers, write the first thing that comes to mind.
Next, picture your ideal day. How do you want to feel? What lights you up? Jot it all down—from sipping your morning coffee to getting ready for bed.
Now tap into what you *really* want to be surrounded by. Love? Freedom? Money? Adventure? Picture what you want around you. Don't water it down and be honest with yourself.
Think about the world you want to create. How do you impact others? What legacy are you leaving? Write that down too.
Visualize another version of you—the one who already has it all. What's their life like? How do they show up? Describe them in detail.
Read it all back and let it sink in. What you just wrote is already planting itself in your subconscious.
Blow out the candle. You've lit something way bigger inside. Keep that energy with you and watch what happens.

Let confidence guide you and determination carry you.
Say it out loud:
I am powerful.
I am confident.
I create my own future.

Write those words down. Put them where you'll see them—on your desk, your mirror, or your phone screen. Let them sink in until they feel like second nature.

WEALTH NOTES

5-MINUTE WEALTH REWIRE

1. Morning Reset
You wake up with your brain still carrying pieces of yesterday's thoughts. Clean them out before your first coffee.
Do this: Write three honest thoughts about money. Be raw. Circle the worst one.
Then flip it immediately.
Examples: "I can't save," becomes "I trust myself to handle money well, starting today."
"I never get ahead," becomes "Money flows to me in bigger ways now."
Why it works: Your subconscious is a sponge in the morning. What you feed it first sets the tone for the day.

2. Midday Check-in
This is when old patterns sneak in. A coworker brags about a raise. A surprise bill hits. Your mind drifts into doubt while driving.
Do this: Stop and take a slow breath. Ask, "What money thought is running this moment?" Spot the sabotage and flip it immediately.
Examples: "This bill is killing me" becomes "Paying this means I'm safe and provided for." "I don't deserve that," becomes "I get to want big things without guilt."
Why it works: It stops old wiring from hijacking your day.

3. Nighttime Wrap-up
Before bed, close the loop. Prove to your mind you are already building wealth, even in small ways.

Do this: Write three wealth-aligned things you did today. Did you speak kindly about money? Did you stop a negative thought? Did you invest in something that grows your income?

Write your rewrites on sticky notes and place them where you will see them often, like your mirror, fridge, or laptop.

Wealth Notes

The Money BFF Audit

- **Talk to your money like it hears you.** Set a regular "money date." Light a candle, pour a beverage of your choice, and open your accounts without spiraling. That's progress, and it builds trust.

- **Clear the shame.** If you wouldn't say it to a best friend, stop saying it to yourself. Everyone makes money mistakes, but you don't need to live inside them.

- **Celebrate the wins, no matter the size.** Paid off a credit card? Did a check-in? Walked past the clearance rack? Own it, brag about it, let it count.

- **Catch the sneaky thoughts.** Notice the quiet "I can't afford that," the whisper "people like me don't," or the loud "this is too hard." Spot it, question it, replace it, and move forward.

- **Stay curious instead of critical.** Ask why you spend the way you do. Ask why saving feels hard, or why success makes you feel guilty. Treat it as information, not judgment.

Healing your money relationship isn't about perfection. It's about partnership and showing up like you're worth it. Because you are.

And each time you do, money responds. It reflects your attitude, matches the energy you give it, and follows your lead into new opportunities.

Wealth Notes

WEALTH NOTES

Wealth Notes

WEALTH NOTES

H

Heal

The release of past hurts, guilt, shame, and money wounds so you can rise lighter and freer toward wealth.

Redefining Your Money Relationship

This next three-part exercise is where things get practical. Take your time with each part. They build on each other, and together they'll reset how you show up with money.

Part 1: Write Your Money Vows:
Write these prompts in your journal or notes so you can come back to them anytime. Say them out loud if that helps also.

- I vow to treat money like a trusted partner, not a burden or a threat.
- I vow to stop avoiding my finances and start showing up, even when it's uncomfortable.
- I vow to speak about money with clarity, respect, and power.
- I vow to forgive myself for past money mistakes and to stop dragging shame around.
- I vow to make decisions that reflect the wealthy version of me—not the scared version of my past.
- I vow to trust that money responds to the energy I give it, and I choose to give it trust, gratitude, and direction.
- I vow to let money support me in building a life I love.

Read them daily and post them where you'll see them. These are your new money vows, declared by the version of you who refuses to play small. You can also add your own vows to this list. Make them personal and specific, so they actually mean something to you. A vow works best when it includes three things: what you choose to stop doing, how you want to show up, and the energy you'll bring to money from now on. When you write yours, think of it like a declaration. You're choosing what ends today and what begins now.

Wealth Notes

Part 2: The Money Check-In

Use these prompts to see how your money relationship mirrors your other relationships. Answer in full sentences for real clarity.

Relationships

Think about how you show up in your closest relationships.
- What qualities make a relationship healthy and empowering for you?
- Which behaviors have no place in a relationship with you?
- How do you know when a relationship feels draining or toxic?
- Do you notice similarities in how you handle people and how you handle money, like avoiding certain conversations or feeling uncomfortable when it gets serious?

Feelings and thoughts

- When you talk or think about money, how do you actually feel?
- Do you feel confident with money, or do you get unsure sometimes?
- Does your attitude about money change depending on who's around?
- How much mental space does money take up for you, and are those thoughts grateful or stressful?

Body check

- Does money mess with your sleep or your appetite?
- What happens in your body when you open your banking app?
- Describe exactly where you feel it and what it feels like.

Wealth Notes

Part 2: The Money Check-In..cont.

Purpose and desires

- Beyond paying the basics, what do you truly want money for right now and later?
- When you picture those wants, what stories or judgments show up?
- How could having more money help you give back or make an impact?
- What legacy do you want your money to build for you, your family, and others?

Vision

- What does your ideal relationship with money look and feel like in your daily life?
- What feels missing right now, and what would have to change to close that gap?
- What is one specific step you can take today to move closer to that vision?

Habits

Review your current money habits with honesty and detail.
- Do you spend fast, save everything, or keep it balanced? What payoff does any of that give you?
- If you save for a rainy day, what good does it do? Does that habit come from freedom or fear? Are you preparing for possibilities or bracing for disaster?
- If you tend to spend quickly, what would shift if you saved more often? How would that feel?
- How does spending honestly make you feel in the moment and how does spending make you feel after?
- What reminders or routines would keep you consistent with money?

WEALTH NOTES

Have a Heart-to-Heart with Money

Picture money sitting across from you looking you straight in the eye. Be direct, honest, and specific.

Ask yourself:
- What have you been avoiding when it comes to money, and why do you think that's continued?
- What are you finally ready to release or heal, starting now?
- How can this partnership grow stronger from here on out?
- When has money already had your back in small or major ways?
- What fun or freedom has money already made possible for you this year?
- Which possibilities excite you when you imagine your financial future?
- How do you want to feel about money from this moment forward, in one clear sentence?
- What promises are you ready to keep showing money that you are serious about this relationship?

This is where your relationship with money starts to shift. It's not just about numbers. It's about building trust, being honest with yourself, and showing up consistently. Money isn't only a tool. It's a relationship that grows stronger the more you show up for it.

Wealth Notes

Part 3: Make Money Your BFF

Treat money like a close relationship and start showing up for it like you mean it.

Try this:

- Think about your favorite person right now. Your partner, your best friend, whoever makes you feel seen and supported. How do you show up for that person, that relationship? Are you present? Do you check in? Do you cheer them on?

- How do they show up for you?

- What do you love about how they treat you or how they make you feel?

- Be honest. How do you treat your money right now? Are you ignoring it? Obsessing over it? Avoiding it?

- If money were your best friend, how could you show up differently starting this week? How would you nurture, respect, and trust that relationship?

- Pick one new action you will commit to this week to prove to your money that you are in it for the long haul. Track your spending, check in, celebrate a small win. Anything counts.

How will you keep yourself honest with this work?

Whatever helps you stay connected, commit to it and follow through. Start small, build the habit, and keep showing up.

Wealth Notes

A simple grounding tool that uses your five senses to shift your focus from anxious thoughts to bringing you back to the present moment

Pick one of these five emotional debts that hits you the hardest and keep it in your awareness.

Notice when shame whispers and answer back with a louder truth.

Notice when guilt pushes you to spend, I want you to pause long enough to hold back.

Notice when fear tightens your chest, breathe until it releases.

Notice when old hurt rises, remind yourself that the past cannot bankrupt your future.

I want you to also notice when unworthiness shows up, and I want you to stand taller while telling yourself that money stays because you say so.

Wealth Notes

Ritual Rendezvous

You've already seen how daily rituals shape your mornings and nights.

Rituals ground you, steady you, and signal to your mind that it's time to shift.

The same idea applies here, only now it's about your money.

This is where you take an honest look at the money practices you already have and decide which new ones you want to bring in.

Think of it as upgrading the way you "date" your money—adding intention, care, and a little spark so the relationship grows stronger.

The point is that your rituals make money care a normal part of your life instead of something you avoid.

- *What's your current money ritual?*
- *What are your favorite money rituals?*
- *What new rituals or bold money date ideas are you curious to try next?*

The way you ritualize money is the way you prove you're ready for more.

Wealth Notes

LETTER TO YOUR LOOT

Part 1: Your Love Letter to Money

- Write money a love letter like you're slipping a note across the desk in class, except this time it's about what you want more of in your life. Keep it playful, keep it light. Tell money what you like about it, and how you'd like things to feel between you. Let it sound flirty, playful, or fun, the way you would if you were teasing a crush.

Wealth Notes

Letter to Your Loot

Part 2: Money's Reply to You
- Now flip it. Imagine money scribbling a note back and sliding it your way. What would it say? How does it feel about the way you've treated it? Let the reply surprise you. Maybe it's grateful, maybe it's calling you out, maybe it's promising more if you keep showing up.

Wealth Notes

Wealth Notes

WEALTH NOTES

Wealth Notes

THE

Unfolding

This is where you bring everything together
and write directly to your future self.

◆———◇———◆

LETTER FROM YOUR FUTURE SELF

This is the final letter in your trilogy.

Fast forward and picture the version of you who fully lives what you've been learning here. Visualize it so clearly you can feel it in every part of you. See the people who surround you, the life you've built, and the version of you who lives this reality every single day.

Write a letter as your future self, speaking directly to who you are today.

Describe what your daily life looks like and feels like in that future, from the way you wake up to how you go about your day.

Talk about what you're doing and how you're living. You can also mention what you stopped doing and what you let go of in your life.

Let your future self tell your now self what's going on, what feels exciting, and how it feels to be wealthy and live from that place every day.

Share the lessons and decisions that carried you here, the ones that changed how you think, act, and decide.

Ask yourself what your future self would thank you for doing right now.

Let this letter be unfiltered and real, something you can return to whenever you need to remember the version of you who already made it. When you finish, read it out loud.

Wealth Notes

Wealth Notes

Your story is unfolding in the best way.

Keep writing it and keep living it.

The future is already yours, and you're ready to claim it.

Wealth Notes

Wealth Notes

Wealth Notes

Wealth Notes

WEALTH NOTES

Wealth Notes

Wealth Notes

CLOSING ENCOURAGEMENT

You've reached the end of this workbook, but this is not the end of your journey. Every reflection, every note, and every exercise you completed here has built the foundation of your aligned wealth identity.

Keep choosing yourself. Keep writing your story. Keep stepping into the version of you who already lives the life you desire.

If you ever need a reminder, come back to these pages. They're here for you whenever you want to realign with your wealthiest self.

I'd love to celebrate your breakthroughs with you. *Follow me* on **Instagram @iamchristinaostroski** and tag me when you share your wins. Together, we'll show the world what aligned wealth really looks like.

You are never walking this path alone.

With Love, Wealth, and Abundance,
Christina

CHRISTINA
OSTROSKI

Christina Ostroski is a respected leader in personal development and wealth mindset, as well as a devoted partner and mother. Her journey from facing the challenges of being a pregnant teen to becoming an acclaimed NLP Trainer, Master Mindset Life and Success Coach is living proof that transformation is possible for anyone ready to rewrite their story.

Christina's approach to wealth and personal growth blends neuroscience, energetics, psychology, metaphysics, quantum physics, and ancient wisdom into practical, powerful teachings that go beyond trends and buzzwords.

With over a decade in the personal development arena, Christina doesn't just teach — she transforms. She certifies and trains new NLP practitioners, EFT practitioners, life coaches, and hypnotherapists, shaping them into skilled leaders. Through her signature frameworks, she helps people break toxic money cycles and claim the wealth and self-worth they were born for. Christina's life and work stand as living proof: with the right tools and deep inner work, transformation isn't just possible. It's inevitable. She proves it daily: you don't just chase wealth. You become it.

www.ingramcontent.com/pod-product-compliance
Lightning Source LLC
Chambersburg PA
CBHW071957070526
44583CB00015B/1235